PUFFIN BOOKS

# The Earthsick Astronaut

The theme for the 1987 *Observer* National Children's Poetry
Competition was 'Planet Earth' and tens of thousands of
children from all over the country submitted an astonishing
number of original poems on a wide range of themes. There
were poems about people and animals, plants and landscapes,
nuclear war and conservation, and the Third World and
politics. Chosen from the top entries to the competition, this
enjoyable collection of poems provides a fresh look at the world
in which we live, drawn with wit, insight and imagination by
the most promising of today's young poets.

The *Observer* National Children's Poetry Competition was
sponsored by the Water Authorities Association and the judges
were Ted Hughes, Janni Howker, Blake Morrison, Sue
Townsend and Wendy Cope.

Royalties from the book go to the charity Water Aid and to
sponsor poetry workshops for children organized by the Poetry
Society.

Selected Poems from the
*Observer* National Children's Poetry Competition,
sponsored by the Water Authorities Association

# The Earthsick Astronaut

*Illustrated by Keith Brumpton*

**PUFFIN BOOKS**

PUFFIN BOOKS

Published by the Penguin Group
27 Wrights Lane, London W 8 5 T Z, England
Viking Penguin Inc., 40 West 23rd Street, New York, New York 10010, U S A
Penguin Books Australia Ltd, Ringwood, Victoria, Australia
Penguin Books Canada Ltd, 2801 John Street, Markham, Ontario, Canada L 3 R 1 B 4
Penguin Books (N Z) Ltd, 182–190 Wairau Road, Auckland 10, New Zealand

Penguin Books Ltd, Registered Offices: Harmondsworth, Middlesex, England

First published 1988
10 9 8 7 6 5 4 3 2 1

Printed and bound in Great Britain by
Cox & Wyman Ltd, Reading

Filmset in 10/12 pt Linotron 202 Galliard by
Rowland Phototypesetting Ltd, Bury St Edmunds, Suffolk

# Contents

## Invisible Treasure

## Skeleton Earth

# Introduction

One of my most vivid childhood memories is of us watching with my friends as the wood behind our house was destroyed. Most of the trees were cut down. But some, including massive oaks, were blown out of the earth with explosives.

When the workmen had gone home we explored the weird moonscape they had left behind. We jumped into craters and swung from branches previously inaccessible to us. But there was no joy to be had in climbing a tree which was lying tamely on its side. Within a few weeks the site was cleared and levelled and there was nothing left to show that our beautiful wood, composed of many different trees and shrubs, had ever existed.

Although I never spoke it aloud I knew what had happened was wrong. Eventually the local authority built houses on the empty site. Mean, squashed-together houses, with tiny gardens. Concrete was the main component of these little houses, so the shouts of playing children echoed harshly and aggressively off the walls. I hated the children who lived in the concrete houses; I blamed them, unfairly, for destroying our wood.

Now, of course, I feel sorry for them because they were never to have the experience of tramping through a snow-whitened wood, or see the first wild flowers appear, or lay on the fresh early summer grass looking up to the sky through a lattice of leaves. They were denied the autumn crunchiness, the scramble for the biggest conkers, the gathering of broken branches for the bonfires. They were never to hear the glorious birdsong at dawn and dusk. But I was lucky and I remember, and the memory still gladdens my heart.

Judging the *Observer* Poetry Competition together with Janni Howker, Blake Morrison, Wendy Cope and Ted Hughes was an immensely pleasurable experience. We argued, read aloud, and occasionally disagreed vehemently about our respective choices. But, in the end there was unanimity when it came to awarding the main prizes.

I think that the poems in this book are quite remarkable. They are passionate and beautifully expressed, and I like to think that the emotions concerning our world and its future are genuine.

We must be forever on our guard – our present government are planning to privatize two hundred and forty nature reserves. Defending this proposed action, a government spokesman was quoted as saying, 'There is far too much sentimental twaddle spoken about conservation'.

I worry that this sinister statement is indicative of even worse to come. In the years ahead I can see us having to defend our national parks and public footpaths. We have already lost many of our hedgerows, and tens of thousands of acres of wilderness have been conifered because certain people are more interested in their own finances than in the general well-being of the land.

Thankfully, this present generation of children seem to be aware and concerned about the need to preserve what is natural and best in our world.

Thank goodness for children, they are our only hope.

*Sue Townsend*, 1988

## Note

Poems marked in the text with an asterisk were all awarded prizes or highly commended in the *Observer* Poetry Competition. A full list of award-winners is given at the back of the book.

# Down to Earth

# The Making of the World

On the first day God made light,
And he was dazzled and made dark,
And then a switch.

On the second day God made the earth
And he took the elements,
Shuffled them,
And dealt them.

On the third day God made plants.
He learnt to breathe the fresh air
Before it was too late,
And he saw beauty.

On the fourth day God made the stars
And God was proud of them.
He winked at them
And they winked back.

On the fifth day God made birds and fish
And wanted conversation,
But they would not talk.

On the sixth morn he made animals to talk to
But they wouldn't listen,
And in the evening he made man.
He said, 'Man, my companion',
And man said, 'Off my land,
You're trespassing.'

On the seventh day God rested
And thought.
And he never saw the eighth day.

*Nick Midgley, 18*

# *Autumn*

Is Autumn what I think it is?

Orangey-red leaves falling off the trees.
Withered summer flowers about to die.
The squashy blackness of ripe blackberries.
And the blurred white greyness of the sky.

The golden golden goldness of Autumn.

The smell of apples freshly picked.
Smoke from bonfires in my hair.
The manure heaps at the allotments.
And the frostiness in the morning air.

The crisp crisp crispness of Autumn.

Football again on the television.
The muffled sounds on a foggy day.
Soft rustling of leaves on the woodland floor.
Cats purring in a contented way.

The quiet quiet quietness of Autumn.

Dark nights getting in your ears.
The clinging dampness of rain.
In the loft the cold wraps around you.
Excitement that you can't explain.

The special special specialness of Autumn.

*Naomi Wratten, 10*

## Planet Earth

Along the long mynd crept, slowly quietly,
my dog and I and the ghostly Roman legionaries.
I stopped at an old Celtic fort
felt like I was betraying my people.
The dog whimpered.
On we went.

There were few sloes.
My hands stained deep purple, aching.
I had nothing but the dog to help me struggle on
like the maid who in her stiff Victorian clothes,
had cried for food while picking sloes.
A terrifying bird swooped down,
its shadow almost knocking me over, a hang glider.

In the next field we threw ourselves down,
in the deep green grass scattered with flowers,
I rolled as far as I could, danced sang and laughed.
The earth was old, but I was still young.

*Caroline Rebecca Murphy, 10\**

# A Midsummer Night's Onomatopoeia

tp.
tp tp.
tp tp thmp.
thmp thmp thMP THMP.
THMP THMP THUMP.
CLUNK.
Can we stop now, dad?
We haven't gone very far, Jo.
Sure. Can I have another mint?
You ate them all.
aw.
Can't you appreciate the country, Jo?
It's boring. I wanna watch TV. It's too quiet.
But if you listen you can
Yeah, yeah, the sounds of nature, I've heard it all before.
Just try it, Jo. Just listen.
aw, gimme a break, dad.
Try it.
awww . . .
shh.
.

.

.

bip.
bipbip.
bipbipbip.
tweeeeeep.
QUARK!
phlaphlaphlaphlaphlap.
mip.
gwurk.
mip.
gwurk.
.

.

bzzzzzzZZZZZZZZZZzzzzzzzzZZZZt.
snapt.
rustlerustle.
bip.
QUARK!
bzzzzzmiddip.
glp.
mip.
QUARK!
zzt.
bipbip.
phlap.
.
.
.

There, y'see? Take time to stop and listen and
Sure. Can we go home now? I'm missing the football game.
OK, Jo. Let's go.
THUMP THMP THMP.
THMP THmp thmp thmp.
thmp tp tp.
tp tp.
tp.
.
.

*Kieran Macdonald, 13*

# A Stormy Night

Strong winds blow
The gales break the glass
In our summer house.
The winds blew
Whoosh, whee, whoo.
Daddy made it new.

*Stuart Fisher, 5*

# Irruption

the sleek streaked wind
quite unsolicited
has come

skewing in through
the holes in
the heart-lace

foaming the grass
like satin
under a thumb

cherry-blossoms
swerve out of nowhere
into my face

*Emma Donoghue, 17*

## Shottisham Common

A road leads down a hill,
then on to a track.
A thin track,
more like a shepherd's path.
The nettles overgrow each side
and our hands go up to shield our faces.
Jess, the dog,
a cross between a greyhound and a lurcher,
slumbers up the path
with no care at all for nettles.
We come out to an open destination,
a brown furrowed field on one side,
like set chocolate sauce
all covered with glycerine icing.
The other side . . .
gorse bushes, blooming with yellow buds
and dotted in between . . .
trees, stark naked,
and around the embedded roots,
warrens, warrens of rabbits,
like footholds in a mountain.
Years ago, when we used to come here,
we hid under trees,
their woody stems draping over
like a shelter covering our bodies.
And then, soon after,
the distant church bell would call out
to say it had found us.
Now the walks we have are different
because I'm growing up.

*Donna Eaves, 13*

# Cart Wheels?

The shafts stand empty:
Wheels that no longer turn.
A tumbrel of yesteryear.

A child sees with open eyes
Beyond deserted wheels,
Beyond the rotting spokes
Where the tall grass whispers.

A horse prances and dances before her,
Waiting to be ridden,
Tamed by imagination
And fed on wishful thoughts.

A jumper transforms into a saddle,
Arms into stirrups;
It creaks with
A smell of leather.

For reins – bailing twine,
Old and frayed.
Now they are ready to gallop
Over picture-book fields.

The world at their feet,
His hoofs pound the ground
In steady rhythm.
They gallop on and on.
Until they can go no further –
They must turn back.

His grey mane plastered with sweat,
Green foam drips from his mouth;
His feetdrag weighted
By sodden clods . . .

. . . An adult returns.
She sees nothing
But a broken, rotting cart wheel
Covered with vicious brambles.

*Gayle Harrison, 13*

# *The Graveyard*

Dull colours,
Sorrow and sympathy,
A boy in a picture,
An unborn baby,
New-bedded soil
On unsettled turf.
A sad tune
With a meaning so true,
A sweet verse,
A white cloth,
A last footstep,
An old vicar,
A plaque on the wall,
A silver cup,
An everlasting candle,
And the carvings of the woodlouse
That, as skilfully as a craftsman's,
Are embedded
In the wood for evermore.

*Simon Honeywood, 11*

# Thaw

Just as the eyes of a child,
who has wet the bed,
will wince and blink under
a white bare bulb when
the sheet is tugged off,

so the earth, wet-eyed,
chill-sodden and sullen,
blinks painfully in the flat
light of the looming sun,
now that the snow has gone.

*Emma Donoghue, 17\**

# The Earthsick Astronaut

He is yearning for his earth senses.
He wants the smell of burning wood to swirl up
And tickle his nose
Like a coarse, rough feather from a bird on the earth;
He wants the sight of a fire,
The flickering fish tails
That make his eyes see nothing else;
He wants to taste bacon, the real bacon,
Tingling on his tongue to evoke
The smell, the sound, the flavour . . .
He wants the touch of cold air on his skin;
Air, a free spirit, teasing, running;
A brush-past kiss on a warm cheek is
His memory;
And then . . . the sad things;
Gravestones like babies' teeth, yet
Decayed with lichen and moss.
But still he is yearning,
Yearning for air, for fire,
For Earth.

*Leonora Dack, 12*

# *Opposites*

The world is full of opposites
Morecambe and Madrid,
Great White Whale and Wallaby
Tadpole and Giant Squid

Tabby Cat and Tiger
Amazon and Nile.
Little furry Monkey
And grinning Crocodile,

Running Stream and Waterfall
Volcano and deep Valley.
Grand broad Highway
And dirty back-street Alley.

Sahara and Atlantic.
Cold Sea with icebergs blue,
Eskimo and Indian,
Wigwam and Igloo

I like the world of opposites
I like the world I see,
I'm glad that everyone in the world
Isn't just like me.

*James Curtis, 11*

# The Rock Pool

I was walking along the beach
When I saw a pool.
The waves were plastic bottles
And the pebbles were bottle tops.
The ripples were silver paper
And toffee wrappers swam around like fish.

Then I remembered a pool
Where the pebbles were solid gold
And the ripples were

Silver stars
And rainbow fish darted
Through crystal water.

*Alex Marples, 8*

# The Night Beach

The tranquil flow of the persistent ever-moving waves
Crashes, tumbles and dissolves into foam on the beach.
The seagulls, above, surf in the pink and grey evening sky
As they screech and listen for a reply.
The hermit crab scuttles along the shore
And disappears into a shallow rock pool hidden from all sight.
The last gulls settle and quieten
And the whole beach is silent
Except for the rumbling of the darkening heavens.
The picturesque reflections of the cliffs of red and white
Hang menacingly over everything.
They are the guardians of the still night beach,
They never fall asleep.

*Vanessa Hedley, 10*

# The Dream of Persephone

Persephone dreams,
Dreams of a meadow
Where nothing is still,
Nothing is sad or lonely.
A giant multi-coloured spotted quilt –
A patch of picture-book poppies
Sways in the wind.
A stronger breeze blows them
And their petals
Turn into thousands of red butterflies.
A cloud forms,
Blotting out the sun,
Leaving a red light.
But soon it scatters
And just long grasses remain.
Slug trails cover a large stone
Like a child's first drawing.
The trees lining the meadow
Have crows' nests on their tops,
Hair with specks of dirt.
And an apple tree grows ping-pong ball fruit.
A brook runs through this paradise
Like a silver ribbon
Binding it up into reality.

*Jane Weaver, 12*

# The Underground Poem

Underground
Thunderground
Listen to the sound
of the African
Elephants

Mud, flood, bud,
blood goes squelchy
in the mud

Little bugs
and worms go
wriggle – wriggle
round
Underground

*Aine Morris, 4*

# The Ants

It's then I miss Zambia
The vast hungry wind
Thrumming the trees
Like musical instruments
Red and dry
Sometimes sucking it to
Writhing dust-devils
Whirling frantically smothering
And evaporating in a lull . . .
(The ants beneath your house
Chew the foundations to powder
And stream up the walls . . .)

Thudding over stubbled grass
Stirring up puffs of white dust and grasshoppers
Rustles in the leaves where
Lizards and snakes warm their cold
Thick blood out of sight
Sudden squalls of tiny birds
Fly together like fists
Opening and closing perfectly together
Never touching . . .
(There are ants in your rafters
And cockroaches in your kitchen.)

Cicadas and crickets tune up
Hoots and chuckles echo out of
Black clumps of bush
The sky is transparent and
Night and stars reflect
In swimming pools
And sewage ponds
And in the sleeping Zambezi
Where, with an idle swing
Of a great grey-green greasy tail

A thousand-year-old crocodile
Rubs a snout of teeth along the rotting body
Of something dead.
(The ants are in your wardrobe
Shake them from your pockets and
Empty your shoes . . .)

Before dawn
Wakes the mother, breast-feeds, cooks
And yawning hoists the baby on her back
Tying him to herself with once bright cloth
And sets out on the eight-mile
Hike to work
Her children sit in the dust
And scratch with the hens
For food and curiosity
(The ants swarm in your hair
And only disperse
When you awake.)

A globe of dazzling sunlight
Drips from a garage tap
Where Coca-Cola crates are piled
Around beggars
A peacock screams

(The ants bite your heels
As you run to the airport.)

*Tanvir Bush, 17*

## No. 7. Sir Ralph Sadler Disappears into the Mist Near Halfway House

Green mist smokes lazily up from the wet grass
    To become pale in the grey air.
The train slides down, crying like a single red lava trail,
    Clicking its cameras like armour plating,
    At the hazy dark crater
Pushing out billows of cloud, like smoke off the lake.
'Moel Siabod' pulls itself up, tired,
Dragging its carriage like a wounded dog
Past the cold walkers
Clutching warmth in their tingling fingers
    At the halfway house.
And 'Yr Wyddfa' passes her in the mist,
    Cameras prickling out like fur on an angry cat
    As they cross, plugging each other's mist slowly,
As if sliding between sheets; to balance,
One relieved on the stone viaduct,
The other clutching tight to the 'Devil's Back',
Like a caterpillar on a tiny twig:
    Crawling to the summit.

*Paul Hodges, 16\**

# The Sandy Shore

The marram grass,
Like pins in a pincushion
Sways to and fro in the wind.
And the sea like thread is slithering and sliding,
In and then out and then in again.
The ringed plover is like a shrunken child
Chasing the waves,
Peeking and poking its little yellow beak here and there.
Swooping and gliding come a flock of kittiwakes.
Although their legs are stubborn on land,
They are excellent for flying,
And they are beautiful birds
With yellow bills like daffodils.
And legs as black as tar.
Snip-snap a pair of pink crabs perform a dance across the sand,
Like scissors to paper.
They prise open the limpets with great
Pride and joy.

*Jason Scoby, 10\**

# Unearthly Proof

'Of course the Earth is flat!'
He doesn't believe me.
'Go to the edge,
And you shall fall.'
He is unconvinced.
He is not interested.
He goes back to playing sumo wrestling.

'Of course the Earth is flat!'
He doesn't believe me.
'Go to the edge,
And you shall fall.'
He is unconvinced.
He is not interested.
He goes back to decorating windows.

'Of course the Earth is flat!'
No one believes me.
'Go back to your basket-weaving,
Continue with your break-dancing.
If you're unconvinced,
If you're not interested,
I will just have to go and prove it.'

'Of course the Earth is flat!'
I'll prove it to them.
Old, crippled, but wise,
I will not heed the heretic voices.
I'd have reached the edge,
Made my name already,
But the years are slowing me down.

'Of course the Earth is flat!'

*Gareth Lawless, 15*

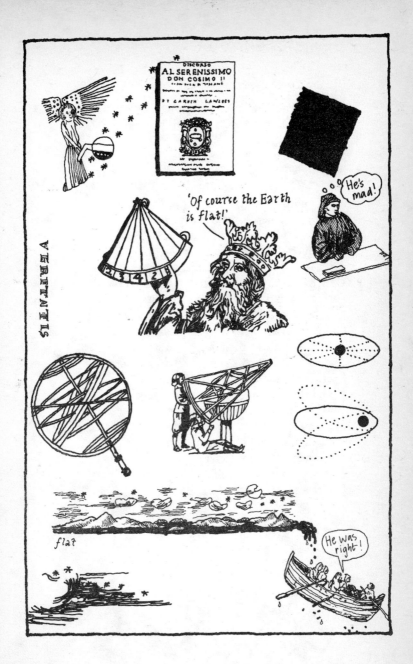

## Earthenware

Tired from walking, doubled like a hag,
And insignificant beside the church,
The weary tinker stops and drops his bag,
Then carefully, as if a leg might break,
Sinks down into the grass beside a stone,
And settles, cursing softly as an ache,
Heats up his legs; he checks that he's alone,
Then guiltily, assured that no one's there,
He opens up his coat and starts to search,
His pockets for a glass of home-made gin,
And touching it, produces with a grin,
A cheap and dirty jar of earthenware,
Dark as the earth it came from, rough to hold,
Fashioned in the kiln but deathly cold,
The tinker rubs a hand around the rim,
Quick, with a jerk, he brings it to his lips,
And downs the rasping liquid at a stroke,
Then, with his dirty sleeve to catch the drips,
Leans back upon the grave and shares a joke,
With his unseeing silent company,
And it's a pleasant touch of irony,
He thinks; that here he sits and jokes and drinks,
With dignitaries and worthies who,
Wouldn't have been seen talking to,
Someone of his kind and so,
He leaves his jar behind and goes.

Clay as the earth around it, rough to hold,
Forged in the fire of love and hard, cold,
Glaze of experience; naked it lays there,
A hollow vessel, empty to the core,
Seeing the world it echoes just the cries,
Of angered magpies startling the air,
Just like a broken mirror, full of lies,
And half-imagined demons and pale fates,
That flit like sombre shadows by the shore,
Of a sunless, murky lake; it waits,
Broken, insolent as a sentenced man,
Unseen but not alone in its decay,
Until the seasons' spangled caravan,
Turns once more and wheels itself away,
And the soft earth rises to claim its own once more.

*Ross Cogan, 16*

# IRA Victim

A second splits before the bullet
Enters the brain,
Exploding in the mind
Like the shattering of a window
Or a waterfall crashing on rocks.

In that split second
He heard his wife putting the peas on to boil,
Saw his children arrive home from school
And throw their coats down in the hall
Just as he had told them not to.
He smelt the dew-scented roses
Colouring his garden,
And the rosehip wine
He had bottled last summer.
He thought of his mother,
Just visiting her neighbour
For a cup of tea,
As she did every afternoon,
And of the tapestry his daughter was making.
And, just before the bullet splintered his skull
And dropped him into the past tense,
He thought of his slaughterers.

The sun shone down on Belfast that day,
Herding black-bodied flies
Around the sticky blood
Spilt like milk on the pavement.
And it's no use crying over spilt milk.

*Siobhan Aiton, 14\**

## The Earth Awaits Us

He was a man
Down to earth,
Free and alone,
Not lonely,
Independent,
Always ready for us.

He was my teacher.
He wasn't old.
He died in school
And nobody saved him.

He was a man I will always remember.
Kind and clever.
For good homework he would draw
In our exercise books, little pictures to please us.

At breaktime in the classroom
He smoked his pipe at his desk.
At Christmas I gave him
A small tin of Old Holborn.

That year we won the cups
For football and netball.
After the match we went to his house,
'The best school teams in the country', he told us.

We raised money for Ethiopia roller-skating.
Our class broke the record.
Our pictures were in the paper,
The only one I've got of him.

He loved his family and his garden.
Weekends he dug the earth.
He talked to us about his flowers
And shared memories of places.

One day he drew in a circle on the blackboard
A dancer turning on a moving dais
To music from *Coppélia* –
We'd been by coach to see the matinée.

After he died we left the picture
On the board for days.
He died in the school play dancing,
Laughing and dancing.

We planted a tree in the earth
In the school field where we can see it
So he would always be part of our lives.
We will always remember him.

They buried him in the earth
By the old churchyard.
The earth is free and alone,
Not lonely,
Independent,
Always ready for us.

*Sophie Benzing, 13*

# Lindow Man

There he lies, an antique in a peat bog,
His face strained with a forced sleep.
Old he lies, a walnut in a peat bog,
A rope coiling round his scrawny neck.
Still he lies, a victim of the peat bog,
His eyes closed like a bolted door.
Sad he lies with mud for a bed,
Reflecting the past, silent and grim.
Sacrificed he lies but no longer bleeding.
Preserved he lies but not new and glistening,
A shadow of himself, only his body left.
But his soul drifted long ago.

*Michael Duggan, 12\**

# Buffalo Men

Stronger than carthorses their massive paws
Hulk a hundredweight of potatoes,
These farmers built like buffaloes.

They roll their calf eyes and pat their stout guts,
These great carcasses of men who stride
In wellies made like tractor tyres.

My blood is the red earth they plant their carrots in.
My roots are ploughed by their harvesters.
These farmers are my ancestors.

The straining wind and itchy woollens
Turn their hides tandoori red,
These big bears with hats rammed on their heads

Who stomp as if through dung or cabbages
And talk like cows chew the cud –
These giant farmers caked in mud.

The mud, my blood, the red, red earth.
My roots chewed by their harvesters.
Farmers, farmers. My ancestors.

Their biceps of beef fork hay to the sky,
Then shake out their earnings from coffee jars
To sit cider-barrel rumps at bars.

Oh where grated red cliffs sink the sunset
And the rooted sea slops liquid gold,
They're men, true men, these buffaloes.

*Katy Daniel, 17\**

## Prayers to the Dead

No man stands
In the white corner she kept
Empty for a secret ornament.
No god is revered
In this house of beige and blue
Where she nightly sleeps.
In the rooms of
Gin and citrus, there are no voices
To convert her to the faith.
And when she prays
It is not to the living empathies
But to the dead.

She sees her prayers
Rising up through the ether, received
By dead perfections.
She turns her back
And these volute offerings descend,
Slowly,
Like feathers unravelling into black tar.

*Imogen Murphy, 17*

# A Man of the Earth

Uncle John lived on the mountain
(not literally you understand);
he would probably die on the mountain too.
From his other home, the softer place,
I could just about make out the eighty-year-old figure
striding bent across the bony thigh of the mountain,
as usual.
His dog was flowing beside him,
circling in front of him, returning,
all was as usual.
Like Finn McCuail he strode
streams, persistent ruins, sucking turf and
knobbed potato pits.
It was his daily ritual – a rapid, fierce assertion
of this as his domain,
this temperamental land of Tavnahoney,
probably coveting the entire glen.
But I was only guessing, I never knew, he never
told me – he thought he was as much a rock
as those tripping his feet.

Later, with the first frown of darkness, he returned,
punctual as ever,
unaffected by the abrasive conditions,
as always.
He seemed gruffly contented with this,
his incapable survey of a dwindling farm.
He eased himself into a grubby, familiar chair
with money and tights lurking beneath its cushions.
Suddenly, he looked old.
I surveyed him with the eye of a stranger,
a city girl as I was.
In his peaked cap, long coat, braces and heavy boots,
he looked curiously fashionable –
fashionable but uncomfortable –

as he always looked when standing or sitting still,
useless.
Lost, he sat in his house, occasionally
wrinkling a fond smile at the pre-bedtime frolics of his grandson
who lisped his new-found words of greeting, though no one had
     taught him –
'By Christ, yon brae . . .' We all laughed.
Pleased, he chuckled from his seat on the cold tiled floor
and looked, almost apologetically, at the red warmth of the
     Sacred Heart
lamp – constant, overseeing and softly approving.

Then, hindered by the slumbering dark,
Uncle John resigns himself to a time –
a short time –
indoors.
In the strict silence he demands, he strains to hear and understand
the television weather report, satellite pictures and all.
Yet, contradictory as ever, he slurps his Guinness loudly, releases
a breath, slurps his Guinness. This action is interrupted only by
a curious popping and slithering from the surface of the hot
     range;
disgusted, I realized he had spat on to it.
His wife didn't flinch, accustomed.
Bottle is replaced by pipe,
worn, friendly and loyal.
With hands grooved by use into the appropriate frame, he cuts
     tobacco
in his hollowed palm,
toughened but not insensitive.
Mechanically, he crams it with his permanently curved finger.
Beneath his nails, persuaded into crevices,
some tobacco fails to reach the pipe and mixes with turf crumbs,
whin slivers, cattle hair
and earth-stubborn Glenaan earth.
A halo of smoke rises;
he has the look of a perfect advertisement for the nostalgic
     modern world.

In broad, creaky yet vibrant tones
he soon begins to chat, talk of sheep sales,
lambing, seasons, change and
neighbours – an interjection by his wife.
He pauses only occasionally, to search his memory.
Drugged by sweet tea and his rising and falling drone, I doze.
As does my memory, I must wryly admit.

This winter things are different:
the painful bleating of the sheep mixes with
that of an ambulance.
The arrival of modernization.
And he never even doted – he hadn't the time.

*Joanne Connolly, 17\**

# Earth

As the glow of the boosters
Floods the sky
The world
Falls away beneath me
Soon the earth cries out
'Come home'
I then felt like a piece of iron
And my home the magnet
The heavens swarm with blackness
Like billions of flies
Looking back
My planet
Seems like a huge glowing emerald
In a black diamond-studded dress
The swirling clouds
Wash from a liner
She was an oasis
In the middle of a black desert.

*Daniel Batley, 11\**

# Memories from Space

I miss the Earth from up here.
Now I see it as a roller
Used for printing patches on newly born cows.
I remember walking through the fields
In which they grazed . . .
The smell of dung, earth, dead leaves and twigs
Was a smell sweeter than honey.
Now missed but before unnoticed.
The leaves, fossilized trees,
And me fossilized within my
          Memories.

*Marie Fenn, 13*

# The Compost Heap

The compost heap
In the graveyard
Hidden from the House of God.
Years of grass cuttings,
The rotting of brown matted grass
To a wet parsley-green.
A tangled cobweb of ivy hides
A cold, stretched-out
Carcass of a chicken.
The dead flowers, unworthy
Now of their place
Over the graves of
Children fifty years old.
The skull of a cat,
Found on the road,
Slung like a hammer
Gripping a daffodil,
A withered stem of life.

*Clifford Black, 12*

# Growing on Earth

When I arrived on this planet Earth
I screamed and shouted
I didn't feed that much
Then I grew and I was one
I learnt to walk on this planet Earth
and how to talk and run
I grew some more until I was two
I had all my injections and so
I could go and swim and play
In the world outside
When I was three
I was horridly bossy
I wasn't very nice
But soon I was four
And I could do more, but
Daddy started going away
To far-off countries
Then we went on holiday too
And saw a lot more
Of this planet Earth
I was five a bit later on
Nice but not perfect
I began to get interested in games
And reading about far-away folk
When I was six, I had friends to stay
And visited my family a lot
I'm seven now and as good as gold
Well, sometimes, I'm told
And I want to know more
About this planet Earth and
The people who lived here before

*Elizabeth Cameron Knight, 7\**

# Invisible Treasure

# A Shrew

A shrew
is fierce.
A versatile sort of chap
with a long pointed nose,
like a pen nib with a black pimple on the end,
which sniffs its way through pebbles, stones or wire netting –
or gives each obstacle a nudge in a temper.
Its long brows hang over its eyes with a sharp look.
It's like water trickling over pebbles in a stream
as it scurries about.
Just bones,
with a short covering of fur and a long pink tail.
The trap goes.
This shrew was fierce.

*Robert Filby, 10\**

# The Black Stallion

His Gleaming, Jet-black hide,
Rippling as he canters over the moor,
His Wild and Unkempt mane
Falling over his neck,
Like an ever-flowing waterfall,
Of Black.

He turns with a snort,
Feeling my Presence,
There is a pause,
As we stare at each other,
He seems to be considering if he should approach,
I look at him,
He sees my Apple,
I hold it out to him,
And he comes.

He pauses, sniffs and bites,
Crunching and swallowing,
The Apple slowly decreases in size.
The Thud of hoofs on grass and turf,
He is charging away.

His Gleaming, Jet-black hide,
Rippling as he canters over the moor,
His Wild and Unkempt mane
Falling over his neck,
Like an ever-flowing waterfall,
Of Black.

*Edward Grace, 10**

# The Rock

The rock is a fist ready to fly out,
Its layers are the skin, the bone and the flesh.

The mountain is a head full of dead but treasured thoughts
About all the creatures and dried-up streams
That used to be.

The range of mountains is a body
Which never stops moving or racing against itself

And the world is a person
Like a figment of the imagination
Impatient to explode.

*Vanessa Hedley, 10\**

# The Dandelion Clock

It is a sheer magic of natural engineering.
Its erect succulent stalk with tiny delicate hairs,
Supporting a feathery intricate filigree of lace.
More involved than a computer,
A cotton-wool ball of complexity,
A thousand different parts united in a marvel
Delicate fluff swaying frantically to and fro
          in the wind like a catkin caught
          in the breeze,
Engulfed in a sea of murky green foliage,
But in one puff, it is gone.

*Richard Adams, 10*

# Field

I had seen the hare twice that summer.
The sleek ears
Draped back over
Mottled fur.

The first time,
The lean body had leapt
From my view
As quickly as an arrow
Loosed from a bow.
When I saw him again
I lay in the grass,
Unobserved,
Under the oak tree.
He sat upright in the field,
His wary eyes watching.
Glass marbles held between fingertips.

And now the lean body
Spread out like the blanket,
Stained with poppy petals.
The wire, flung to one side,
Knots in a piece of string.
The patches of darkness,
Of death,
Creep over the lifeless body.

I turn my head away.

*Rachel Gardam, 13*

# The Wandering Tree

Your hands seize the sprawling haze.
You slump, though your arms flicker
       through the daunting dusk.
Your roots are torn and burnt,
And your bark flutters through the echoing drains.
Searching blindly, fingering the bald
       leaves that droop
       down your spine.
Calling alone your branches split,
Cracking at your snapped palm that falls to your feet.
Your shoulders collapse and spring through the scarred, torn
    leaves.
Dust buries your dangling hair, as you search still.
But as you're cut down your remains
Start to touch and search through the dawn.

*Lisa Dixon, 10*

# The Dull Potato

The potato,
Lying on its side,
Eyes staring,
Everywhere.

*Keeley Saunders, 10*

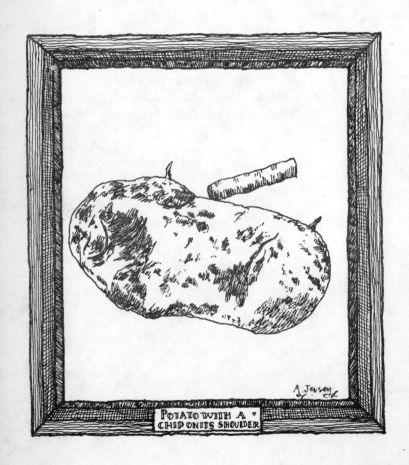

POTATO WITH A
CHIP ON ITS SHOULDER

## The Mole

The mole, a shadow of the night,
A ship of the underground,
Unsinkable,
Unstoppable,
Weaves through oceans of dirt.
His trademark,
Half a globe;
The solid half of the world is his.

The mole heap
Is only the tip –
Underneath, a network of pipes
Which carry
Black ships with worms as cargo.
These sailing ships convert into
Battleships who fight against the Earth.

*Robert Adcock, 11*

# Mole Trapping with Grandad

The heavy thump of hobnail boots
And the sharp retort
As a moling-stick strikes a flint.
You can feel the soft lack of earth
As you push a stick
With a quick jerk into a tunnel . . .

Then, the grind of the jaws
As they slowly open and click into place.
Tiny droplets of dew
Slide off the grass
As the turf is lifted
And the trap is slowly pushed in.
And you catch a whiff
Of stale air as it forces its way out.

Then sitting, after setting a good number of traps,
Under my favourite oak,
Eating a packed lunch,
And leaning back to look at nests
As they sway and rock in the wind . . .
I wonder if they get seasick.

Then, it's back off to the well-remembered spot
To dig up the trap, to see a dead mole,
A cold, forgotten pair of ear muffs,
Lying limp in my hands.
I suddenly push it into the bag.
I shrug and tell myself,
Never again.

*Matthew Line, 11*

# Death of a Mole

A furry drawstring purse
Wobbles through the field.
Blind in the upper world
But a ruler downstairs.
Its body black
But its nose brown from furrowing,
All its tunnels dug out gently,
Not ploughed like a bulldozer.
The calm pace of its scuffing
Makes it a genteel ruler.
The mole is not a savage,
But dinner coils past,
The purse opens
And dinner rolls into the inner lining.
Hunger satisfied,
The mole scurries on up to our world,
Blind again.
The farmer has his shovel;
The guillotine descends.

*Matthew Shepherd, 12\**

# The Old Chicken

The old chicken cackled
Like an old woman,
Her beak strung open,
Gasping for air.
Her eyes,
Like deep holes in her head,
Sunken and dull.
She blinked, slowly, in the dim light.
Eyelids flicked down, and up again,
Thin flaps of skin,
Like scales of a snake.
Her crimson crest flopped over her left eye
Like a red beret.
The wattle, a double chin
Or a pink scarf,
Flapped as she turned her head.
Scaly legs,
Like the body of a worm,
Fold and wrinkle and loose flaps of skin.
Tail feathers overlapping one another
As a fan of cards.

The old chicken gargled softly
As if trying to sing herself to sleep.
Then pecked slowly in a puddle in front of her.
The barn was dark,
But a patch of light lit up the two hen boxes in which she lay.
Her neck hung out of the box
Like a dog's tongue from its mouth
And dangled limply in the puddle.
Her eyes closed, as if still sleeping.
She gargled no more.

*Sally Clifton, 12*

# A Worm's Eye View

I like eating my way
through the soil
I do not like the sharp
blade of a spade
I love wet grass.
I hate a bird's nippy beak.

*Ross Callister, 7*

# I'm a Worm

I'm a worm
I live at Stonehenge
So people can't trample me

I feel the earth it is soft and warm

I do not know much about the earth or about people

I feel what I am
Safe, comfortable and free.

*Ben Kay, 9\**

# Worms

A worm comes wriggling
through the earth
as if it's been buried,
its dark purple body
stained by blackberry juice,
lines every little way
as if you could pull it to pieces
like an orange in segments.

Lines move in, out, in, out,
as if it's trying to pump out
blackberry juice.
Veins are grey and look brittle.
Here comes another one.
His head lifts
under a clot of mud.
His one big purple muscle
refuses to move.

Then the body
trickles along the earth . . .
but now he lies
perfect in my memory,
the stained worm, dead.
The worm earthed –
the blood-clotting movement dead.

*Lorraine Dixon, 12\**

# Dog on the Dung Heap

I saw the dog.
An Irish terrier,
Snared and caught
In the metal door
Of a rat trap.

Its leg hung limp,
A sliver of skin
Pulled away,
A pocket,
Ripped away from the coat.

'It'll have to be put down,' my father said.
I waited.
'Well, go on then. Go away!'

The next day
I found the dog.
It was lying on the dung heap,
Comfortably,
As though asleep.

Its fur was matted
Around its chest,
But not with mud.
Blood was scattered
In a haywire circle,
As if someone had dropped
A glass of red wine
On to a furry carpet.

I ran . . .

*Jude Fitzgerald, 12*

# *September 15. Dog Died. (Topsy)*

I stood watching
As she slobbered and panted
Her liquid eyes begged
So my mother hid her face
As I nodded to the vet
Who harpooned her
As I stood watching
Just like television
I switched off and walked away.

It was only a damned dog
No feeling, no soul,
The big boy said to me.
I slept, while kids and dogs
Died everywhere.
Next day got up,
Ate breakfast, patted Bet,
Kissed mam and walked to the big school
To learn from books about dying
As Bet sat on the grave
And cried.

*James Williams, 18*

# Autumn Squirrel

A last look at the earth,
As I enter the hollow tree;
Inside, the nuts which I have collected,
Ready to eat.

Meanwhile outside,
A blanket of leaves forms on the ground.
The sky darkens
And a black beast fills the air.

The leaves drop off the tree one by one,
Like drops of rain falling off the branches.
The toadstools, half demolished
Ruins of a castle.

The moss on the tree
Like a soft punch bag;
The roots of a flower loosen
Like a slackened tooth . . .


Now I must sleep away the winter.

*Luke Chaplin, 11*

# Hibernating Dreams

I must sleep. . .
I don't know why. . .
I sink down down down down
To dream of leaves of fire
And apples rotting.
I smell the musty smell
Of wet leaves,
The trees shedding their last few flames of life
Before sleeping. . .

The misty evenings of warm autumn days,
A sensation of mouth-watering
Bugs and beetles.
The leaves that fall
Are falling to death,
Falling from a forgotten tree.
Everything is but a skeleton of
What was once a wonderland.
Autumn is a dead memory of days gone by.
Here I sleep in my tent of warmth,
While outside
Frost-lace crochets the world.

*Emma Fensom, 11*

## Invisible Treasure

Millions of decades ago,
Before dinosaurs lumbered,
Tiny microscopic creatures lurked,
With beady eyes peering at you,
Asterionelle and Cyclops peered,
From swampy marsh,
Jungle all around you,
The Invisible Treasure not yet found beneath rock?
Sedimentary!
Igneous!
Metamorphic!

*Nicholas Ramsden, 8*

# Old Man Cactus

The old man cactus is covered in long snow-white hair
But he has no eyes to see with, no ears to hear with,
And no mouth to speak with.
Yet in his own mind
He knows the world that walks past his window-sill.
For old man cactus is wiser than the trees.
He learnt long ago how to live in the hot yellow deserts
Where no other plants survive.
With great cunning he covered his back in cruel spikes –
No creature could bite him open or drink his blood.
He knew the great heart of the sun
And the long cold stab of the night.
But old man cactus survived them all:
He sat in his dry hot bed
Waiting for someone to come. . .
And they did in time.
They pulled him from his socket
And put him into a warm moist bed.
From thereon he lived for years and years,
Growing his beard longer and longer.
Happy to sit in the sunshine
And happy to watch the rain fall down past his window-sill.

*Joanne Drake, 13*

# Skeleton Earth

# Planet Earth

God was sitting in His garden, in the evening, with His gin
(For the joys of creativity were wearing rather thin)
He had drafted out the Universe, and calculated π
Then He saw a barren, blue-green ball suspended in the sky.
'I'll create a whole new planet with high mountains and deep seas,
And a billion different life-forms from great dinosaurs to trees,
And the balance will be perfect, Nature's harmony
    complete –
Until I create a primate that walks upright, on two feet.
These said creatures shall be jealous – they'll make wars and want
    to fight,
They will have a sense of logic, so they can't tell wrong from right.
Out of all the different life-forms there, they'll be the most
    confused,
With their things they call "society" and even "moral views".
I shall colour them in every hue, from black to milky white,
They'll play games of "race relations" and of "basic human
    rights",
And so that they haven't got a hope of knowing what to do,
I shall make them eleven sexes but say there are only two.
I will give them "state economies" and drugs to dull their minds,
So that they think they know about the safety of mankind,
While their world expires around them, and the sands of time run
    dry,
While the piles of deadly weapons rear against the clear blue sky.'
Then God broke off, for the thought somehow did not appeal to
    Him
Of a planet's own destruction – so He polished off His gin,
But the thought was not forgotten, for, before the sun had set,
God had catalogued Earth's blueprint in His filing cabinet.
And, there, on His coloured memo pad (with ball-point, done in
    red)
The clear headline 'Eve and Adam' could quite obviously be read.

*Sarah Sarkhel, 16*

# Irish Indians

If we could put our ears
Like Indians, to the green flatness
Of rain-soaked ground,
And hear not only the thin soft babble
Of earth-cooled running streams,
Or marshy foot
Of enemy
Approaching,
But . . .

The tumultuous gurglings
Of the bubbling earth,
Casting and grinding
Like a swirling sea –

First we would hear
The growing –
Squeal of sproutings
And the rush and hiss of filling sap

And next,
The wrenching –
Retch of rooted things
Pulled from dark and swollen earth

Air thick
With clammy gaggling
Muggy fog
Of birth and dying . . .

If we could put our ears
Like Indians, to the green flatness
Of rain-soaked ground –

We would build our Silence Stations
High
In the thinness of the
Sparse
Blue
Sky.

*Jenny McCartney, 16\**

# *Status Quo* or *The World as It Is*
## A Satire

I knew a man who feared the earth would grow
So large, it would forever fall, and so
Cause man's destruction. Wishing to prevent
This possible catastrophe, he meant
To wear away the earth with walking. But
His trouble started here.

His friends, when asked if they would aid his cause,
Were mainly shocked at first – some thought that he
Was joking, afterwards that he was mad
As it grew clear his proposition was
In earnest. Some professed they shared his fear,
Howe'er, their answers all were negative,
Whatever the reactions, and the man
Was left alone
To wear away the earth.

His cause attracted public notice, though
Whilst busy walking on the Southern Downs,
Which, being chalk, erode more easily,
He was discovered, somehow, by the press
Who found him trivial enough for print.
Thus he was publicized and ridiculed.
In spite of this, some claimed discipleship,
And joined him on the hills
In mass erosion.

The government grew worried. Scientists
Predicted doom, should some decrease, though slight,
In volume, mass and gravity of earth
Disturb the subtly balanced solar system.
Economists predicted heavy loss
In mining, quarrying and agriculture.

The military feared their secret bases'
Discovery, as they were underground,
And archaeologists bemoaned the fate
Of all uncovered evidence. Even
The Churches, Catholic and Anglican,
Condemned the man's attempt, and deftly used
The first verse of th'eleventh chapter, 'Proverbs',
To justify their ethical position.
With pressure such as this from ev'ry side
The government had quickly to decide
Upon some course of action, to suppress,
With ev'ry means, the source of this distress.

And, therefore, surreptitiously, police
Of some high order – Special Branch perhaps,
Removed th'offending subject to a cell
Where he might be successfully restrained.
But there he still continued with his plan
By pacing round relentlessly. They strapped
Him tightly to a bed, but even then
He shook until its castors rubbed the floor.
Without most direful inhumanities
It seemed impossible to stop this fiend –
And governments have morals, though they may
Be spare and flexible, and seldom shown.
And thus they bargained with him: 'We will let
You free to concentrate upon your work,
But only at the granite Aberdeen,
And under constant watch.' Reluctantly
Did he assent to this.

Upon his swift release, the man did find
Himself the centre of a nation's scorn:
The press's view of him having evolved
From one of ridicule to one of hate,
Depicting him as some Asmodeus
And his disciples as diabolists.
At Aberdeen he was abused by mobs,

The 'constant watch' ignoring this the while.
His followers had guessed correctly at
The circumstances of his disappearance,
But, worn with persecution and with walking,
And fearing *their* imprisonment, they kept
Their silence, and abandoned their great cause.
Therefore, alone, completely without friends,
He resumed his wearing.

This all was years ago. A Commons' bill
To ban 'malign perambulation' is
At present, under scrutiny, and will
Assuredly, attain the Lords' consent.

My friend, as he has since become, is ill
And slowly dying. He contracted some
Most fatal foot disease, peculiar
To Aberdeen. Unfortunately, there
Is no known cure. He had no kind of shoes,
Because, with dole, he could no way afford
To keep replacing those the earth destroyed.
His feet are badly blistered, covered with
A layer of 'Squameus Epithilium'.
I went to visit him in hospital.
He sits upright, quite still, upon his bed
Too weary, far, to move, and looks without
His window all the day, with terror, at the earth expanding.

*Brian Mitchell, 17*

# *Jigsaw World 4" × 10"*

A little girl sits at the table, small box underarm,
She opens the box and tips out the pieces.
Thinks hard, finger in mouth,
Carefully, puts piece next to piece on to the table,
Edge to edge, slots into place,
Until the finished product's there,
She stands back with a smile on her face,
It shows a picture of green landscape,
People, animals, fish and fowl,
Pleased with what she's done,
She sits back, but doors slam,
Brother pushes past,
Bad-tempered, violent and sharp.
Pushes the pieces off the table.
Which lie broken, forlorn on the floor.

*Rachel Gibson, 14*

# A Bright Future?

Twinkle, Twinkle, little Earth,
How I wonder what you're worth.
Chopping forests by the score,
Soon we won't have any more.

Twinkle, Twinkle, planet fair,
What is happening in your air?
Acid rain and airborne lead,
Pretty soon we'll all be dead.

Twinkle, Twinkle, on the sea,
Floating oil and foul debris.
Sewage floating by the shore,
Killing bathers by the score.

Twinkle, Twinkle, planet blue,
Animals are going too.
Chemicals and pesticides,
Causing deaths and suicides.

Twinkle, Twinkle, disco star,
Getting noisier by the bar,
Concorde's roar and jumbo jet,
And it's getting noisier yet!

Twinkle, Twinkle, earthly light,
Glowing brightly in the night.
Caesium, plutonium,
Radon and uranium.

Twinkle, Twinkle, in the sky,
Watch the cruising missiles fly.
Fire a laser, drop a bomb,
Now all the pollution's gone!

*Andrew Dawson, 12*

# *The Way I Would Make the Earth*

One day I'd peer down into space,
And find it very big,
With nothing there
Just like a football stadium that finished an hour ago,

So I'd get a light bulb
And shape it like a beach ball,
And colour it bright orange
Like a car's signal light,
And then there's a black side,
Like a Midland bank bag,
So I'd get a newspaper,
And crunch it up and rip it up,
And throw the paper at the black
Like hitting a rounders ball miles away.

Then I'd think a bit,
And sigh a bit,
And ping a little bell would sound,
Like a Hanford prep bell,
So I'd get a task book,
And make the Earth,
Then put some ink into the holes,
So that would make the sea,
And then some brown and white leather
And make man just like me,
Tho' none can come and see me,
But my favourite thing of all,
Is a bird with wings so bold as the sun.

*Alexandra Wilson, 10*

# Monster

The Earth Monster
    crawled into our kitchen
        yesterday morning.
    Slunk belly-grovelling
        rubbling and
        gravelling.
I heard its
    acorn-knuckled rattle
        upon our table
        where it sat,
    its snake-black
        trunk-thighs
    splitted
        moist
        with whitish
        close-clumps
    of mushrooms swollen
        there.

Everyone stared at
        the strange face of Earth:
    the blushed clay-jowls;
    the rose lips
        slippery with fresh rain;
    the frown of furred
        rusted moss,
and behind glossy crocus-lids,
    two pure,
        mulberry
            round eyes.

If you carved Earth
　　into halves
　you'd find its organs:
a pulsing squash of
　pale gold;
two jellied
　　naked lychees;
　　a pink muscular guava;
　and a heart,
　　as tough-skinned
　　as sweet-blooded
　　as beetroot.

When Moon was
　pin-curled pretty
on night-time's silent shoulder,
　Monster crept from our kitchen.
　I think it will come again
　　one day,
　　to cuddle us
　　in those
　　shyly lustrous
　　silver-boughs.

*Ottilie Hainsworth, 17\**

## Skeleton Earth

He came, waving bones at me one night,
Tapping out jigs on the back of his palms,
But they weren't the bones of men –
Manageable things: that live, die,
And return, hunched in the corner
Of doctors' waiting rooms,
Vanishing at cock crow.
These bones have finality,
One can tell they're here to stay . . .

'Sir, there is a roundness and emptiness about you
That belies your stringy temperament;
Your openness astonishes me.
Things of the world are generally obscure,
But I can see through you –
Transparent as the day.
Is that a star, sir, shining through the space
Where your liver used to be?
And upon your head – I must admire it –
A coronet of thorns?
It is!
My, the poignancy with which your sufferings fill me,
You must have been a martyr or a saint;
An emulation of Our Saviour. With one difference,
All your blood has drained away.
Excuse the question, sir, who drank it?'

'Bogmen from the East, my dear.
They found my soil absorbing.
Not only that –
My extra things: all my little jewellery of rivers and forest sap
Were requisite.
They picked cherries from my mountains for their hats,
Drew world maps with my fingers,
And shot Gurkhas with my eyes.

One or two small things they were wise enough to ignore –
This delicate filigree of tree roots you see, girdling my waist.

'Have you seen those Chinese ivory balls –
One inside another,
Encompassing a mysterious perfection?
Ah well; I was the error, the deviant,
The one they forgot to fill.
No one had any stomach for me after that,
So they left me:
Rolling around on an ivory chessboard
Without any pieces,
Under a dark blue sky,
                    On the deep waters.

'One night at Christmas time, I will return;
Oak trees and narcissi falling from me like powder.
When I laugh, men shall be clothed in gold,
And when I love, wires shall break.
I tell you the truth;
They will bleed tulips when I come!'

. . . He, dancing, missed his footing,
And shrieking, fell.
This ball of roots and leaves and things,
Lay scattered like egg shell.

*Kirsty Whitehead, 18*

## 4.00 What's that?

Radiation
Fiona Benjamin
with ANTONY, DEREK, IAN,
KATRINA, CIARIA and KENNIE
Story: The glowing train
by PETER WILSON
Illustrations by KEITH BROWN
Storyteller JUDY DAVIS
Musical director BARRY MANILOW
Producer KIRK DOUGLAS
Executive producer
LLOYD COLE

## 4.10 Ratman

starring Roland Rat Superstar
and Edward Shevardnarze
as 'Mr S'.
The Case of the Low-flying
Industrial Pollution
Important people are being
forced to breathe in $CO_2$
Where is it coming
from?
Police chief JACK WARNER
Written by IAN BRUMPTON
and WILLIAM SHAKESPEARE
Assistant producer ERNIE BONDS
Producer DONALD FARFRAE

## 4.20 Mutants

The Windscale factor

## 4.40 Flee with me

Presented by Bruno Brookes
MR EINSTEIN and DIBBLESDALE
COUNTY SECONDARY SCHOOL
are today's challengers
to be the last ever to take
part? Who will survive the
Holocaust Round?
Devised by BIG BANG PRODUCTIONS
Producer HUMAN BOB

## 4.55 Newsround

with Finnish Roger
Helen Roller-Coaster
and John Raven
Newsround brings you the
end of the world and why
it's happening
Editor CLIFF HANGER

## 5.05 Red Peter

with Chicken Curry
Corion Fleeing
and Vet infielding
news of the 'old spaceships'
Christmas appeal
Editor RAN AWAY

## 5.35 Martyrteam

Presented by Angel Dripping
Question one: When will
the world end?
Answer: Any minute
now.
Question: Then what are
you doing here, you mad
fools?
If you want to be just as
silly, don't try to escape
watching tonight's edition
of Martyrteam
Assistant producer
JOHNNY THUNDER
Executive producer CLARE LIGHTNING
Director RAY GUN
Producer IRMA GEDDON

## 6.00 Six O'Clock News

Fiona Armstrong
and Keith Brumpton
with the latest pictures
from the end of the world.
All times approximate
hereafter
Weather DISTURBED

## 6.25 Gary Glitter

A farewell special, live
(we hope) from Blackpool
Tower, with many of your
favourite stars, including
Andromeda, The North Star, Perseus.
Producer LAST ONE OUT THE DOOR

## 7.00 - ? Wotan

Join Terry and any other
survivors in the special
'life pod' as they discuss
the days events

## IBC 4

## 2.17pm End of the world

Live coverage from Berwick
of the address by the
President of the United
States, and debates
including topical motions
such as imprisoning those
responsible
Commentators
ROBIN DAY, DAVID DIMBLEBEE
Producers MEL BROOKS
and ARTHUR MILLER
Engineering Managers
NASA
Conference Co-ordinator BILLY WHIZZ
Editor IRMA KUTZ
including the
3.00 News and Weather

3.50 Victim count
Regional News and Whether...

## 4.00 Championship Bowls

Further coverage with DAVID
VINE of the last ever
British Open. Can DAVID
BRYANT overcome last years
champion, FRANK DRAKE,
on his home ground, here
in Plymouth?

## 6.00-7.30 Future World: The Day the Earth Stood Still

FILM Opens and closes
a season of science
fiction films.
Today starring
Desmond Lynam
in a remake of the
original 1951 movie.
In this new version, Des
stars opposite Gyles
Brandreth and Sarah
Green
Out of space comes the
worlds most civilized alien
to warn mankind of the perils
of war. Can the visitor
overcome the suspicions of
the world's leaders?
Klaatu DESMOND LYNAM
Helen Benson SARAH GREEN

# A Lesson

The End of the World will be filmed
Thirty times over.
And given the 'Comment' part on Channel 4.
The End of the World will be
A theme tune
A book
A film
A T-shirt
And an hour-part drama serial
Covered on 'Did You See?'
The End of the World will be a poster
On every slab of rubble
To remind us all of the power
We possessed,
The power we abused.
The End of the World will be reviewed
By a best-selling author
And shown on 'Bookmark'.
The End of the World will be broadcast
Throughout a nation
That's been dead
For thirty years.
The End of the World will be a lesson
To us all.
But none of us will learn.

*Sinead Morrissey, 14*

# Just Another Planet

Her body was found this morning, wrapped
In a white sheet by the side of the road. Police say she had been
Stabbed at least twelve times with a blunt instrument
And there were also signs that

Oh whoops I've dropped my sandwich on the floor. Mother!
MOTHER! I've dropped my sandwich what shall I
Do? Can I have a cloth MOTHER have you been

Executed by Tamil separatists. The Sri Lankan Government
claims
The people were backed against the wall and shot one by
One apparently without discrimination although it seems that

I've got most of it up. Can
I have another one please? And
An apple, thanks. What's the time? Almost six. Damn I want
To ring John as soon as he gets in. What a BORE! What a

Terrible explosion, releasing a cloud of radioactive dust
Over most of the country. This is the
Second major accident at the plant
This year and a total of fifteen people are thought to have
Died in the blast itself or from the massive doses of
Radiation they received. A spokesman for the company said

Come on, John, where are you? Get a move on. O God
I've bitten my lip. This is TOO much. What's the matter with
My teeth anyway that they can't

Have died in a coach crash
In France. Eyewitnesses claim the coach appeared to jolt slightly
Before it rolled over, and burst into flames
With at least six people trapped
Inside. It appears that

This apple is soft. O Lord WHAT
IS WRONG with life today? I should never
    Have got out of bed this morning. I knew
As soon as I did that

    England have been beaten one-nil in
A friendly with Sweden. The goal
    Came in the thirtieth minute from a shot by

    God! That is AWFUL! That is APPALLING!
I can't believe it! What is the
    MATTER with those idiots I dare say LIFE I ask you. . .

*Gregory Sly, 15*

# There Is No More

The crops are all dead.
The land is burnt dry.
There is no more water.

The farmer is defeated.
His family go hungry.
There is no more food.

Walking for miles.
Nowhere to go.
There is no more home.

They arrive at the camp.
Half dead and tired.
There is no more hope.

A world split in two.
The rich and the poor.
There are no more equals.

*Richard McKenzie and*
*Chris Barrett, 11 and 10*

# This Is Where Your Money Goes

They crawl on their bellies
Through the dust and scorching morning sun . . .
To drink mud,
Tepid brown ale that even spartan Adam would have shunned.
No Auschwitz silence (although the scenes are similar),
The tribe wails as one baby,
Trying to stay thirst by chewing on leather breasts.
Eyes, sunk like dry empty wells
Stare out, hope windswept by burning sand.
There is no water for straws to float,
No vain frantic clutchings of the doomed.
Sunk even to such desperation they 'live' still,
From the rumour of one day to the next,
Remembering the day it rained seven years ago.
Stark skeletons cauled in parchment,
Their lethargy tiring them,
Even their sores have no energy to run.
The after-death could match no hell as this.
The dying innocently question the justice of their suffering,
And in our security we drink deeply,
Savouring the answer in our faith.
Charities pluck the notes of conscience,
A song to save a nation of people with mouths
Too dry to sing their own anthem.
Aid buys bullets.
They cannot drink blood,
Theirs is cupped in your hands.
A hundred children die at this full stop.

*Peter George, 17*

92

# God's Suffering Children

God's children,
Wearing rags.
Suffering badly,
No clean clothes
To put on.

God's children,
Drinking infected water.
Dying of thirst.
Lots of little insects
Flying around.

God's children,
Living on the dry land.
Dusty river banks,
Not many crops
Are growing.

*Elizabeth Johns, 11*

# Of Her Changing

Unblurred through grey years of her changing,
he recalls what is not found:
mother, earth in scabs
tensed upon his legs,
sighs and smiles and beckons.

Numb now, in the water stands.
From skin that is scoured bruised broken with cuts
she strokes the mud to streams
rilling into the bowl.
Finds himself again,
steps from dimness, which she takes,
throws, a moment's whiteness,
a brief unsteady gull
lost in a scamper of drops.

So she bathed him as a child.
So she was bathed upon a wild,
needle-teething coast –
wide and unworn, thumped by waves –
and laved in green of woods
where she could wander fields,
with gladness in earth's suck and grit.

But there is silence in her eyes
where questions pool and rock.
The grown child will despise
the grey dregs of her hair;
and she will sometime wake
on rubble of herself,
the landslide at her throat.
She knows what curtains coal-dust draws
on waters of the font;
and not all shifted falls to place.

She fears her strengthless hand
may not stroke pain out like a crease
or bear his sins within a bowl.

*Francis Thompson, 18\**

# A Drink of Water

The tinkling rippling
water in the tap.
The smooth calm water
in a glass.
The water in my mouth
feels like foam and froth.
The popping bubbles in the bath.
Water is amazing, it keeps me alive.

*James Barnes, 7*

# Hot, Dry Dust

Dust.
Hot, dry.
Very thirsty.
Polluted waters,
Rivers killing them.
Lots of dead plants and trees.
Not much food growing.
Thin as a rake.
So hungry.
Hot, dry.
Dust.

*Barbara Johns, 11*

## The Eyes of the Past

Lying deathly still on a busy, bustling motorway is a hare.
His beautiful, sleek coat is as soft as God's pillow,
His long, delicate ears are still pricked and his nose still wet,
His eyes catch the light and reflect the past,
Green pastures, unpolluted streams and golden cornfields.
The hare's legs are outstretched as if he is begging for life,
Does anybody care that his world is slipping away?

*Rebecca Martin, 10*


## Our Children

Africa.
Starving to death.
Some can't carry their heads.
A bowl of maize a day.

Africa.
All they own is a bowl and some rags,
Flaps of skin like a folded piece of paper.
And half a head of hair.

*Timothy Peters, 9*

# Lists of prize-winners

### Age group: 10 years and under

1st prize *Planet Earth*  Caroline Rebecca Murphy
2nd prize *A Shrew*  Robert Filby
3rd prize *The Sandy Shore*  Jason Scoby
Highly Commended *Growing on Earth*  Elizabeth Cameron
    Knight
*The Rock*  Vanessa Hedley
*I'm a Worm*  Ben Kay

### Age group: 11–14 years

1st prize *The Earth Awaits Us*  Sophie Benzing
2nd prize *Death of a Mole*  Matthew Shepherd
3rd prize *IRA Victim*  Siobhan Aiton
Highly Commended *Worms*  Lorraine Dixon
*Lindow Man*  Michael Duggan

### Age group: 15–18 years

1st prize *Buffalo Men*  Katy Daniel
2nd prize *Thaw*  Emma Donoghue
3rd prize *Skeleton Earth*  Kirsty Whitehead
Highly Commended *Monster*  Ottilie Hainsworth
*No. 7. Sir Ralph Sadler Disappears into the
    Mist Near Halfway House*  Paul Hodges
*Irish Indians*  Jenny McCartney
*Of Her Changing*  Francis Thompson

## School prizes

Halesworth Middle School
Suffolk

*Teacher*: Jill Pirrie

Poems submitted by the school included:

*Cart Wheels?* Gayle Harrison
*Shottisham Common* Donna Eaves
*The Graveyard* Simon Honeywood
*The Earthsick Astronaut* Leonora Dack
*The Dream of Persephone* Jane Weaver
*Memories from Space* Marie Fenn
*The Compost Heap* Clifford Black
*A Shrew* Robert Filby
*Field* Rachel Gardam
*The Wandering Tree* Lisa Dixon
*The Old Chicken* Sally Clifton
*The Mole* Robert Adcock
*Mole Trapping with Grandad* Matthew Line
*Death of a Mole* Matthew Shepherd
*Worms* Lorraine Dixon
*Dog on the Dung Heap* Jude Fitzgerald
*Autumn Squirrel* Luke Chaplin
*Hibernating Dreams* Emma Fensom
*Old Man Cactus* Joanne Drake

## Water Aid Trophy

Whitstone Junior and Infants School
Devon

*Teacher*: Ian Alexander

Poems submitted by the school included:

*Our Children*  Timothy Peters
*There Is No More*  Richard McKenzie and Chris Barrett
*God's Suffering Children*  Elizabeth Johns
*Hot, Dry Dust*  Barbara Johns


## Certificates of Merit

*Age group: 10 years and under*

Richard Adams, Toby Baker, James Barnes, Richard Bath,
Francis Bennett, Ross Callister, Catherine Clarke, Ben Curtis,
Lisa Dixon, Stuart Fisher, Hannah Futter, Edward Grace,
Sakbeer Kaur, Maeve Anne Lagan, Alex Marples, Rebecca
Martin, Suzannah Jane Miller, Aine Morris, Susanna Paden,
Timothy Peters, Nicholas Ramsden, Keeley Saunders, Sharon
Tooke, Timothy Warnes, Alexandra Wilson, Naomi Wratten.

*Age group: 11–14 years*

Juan Manuel Aguirre, Daniel Batley, Katharine Scarfe Beckett,
Sally Clifton, James Curtis, Leighton Davis, Andrew Dawson,
Rachel Gibson, Darren Hobbs, Novak Ivanovic, Jamie Latter,
Kieran Macdonald, Sinead Morrissey, Emma Smith, Michael
Stammers, William Taylor, Deborah Ward, Mandy Wordingham.

*Age group: 15–18 years*

Jenny Alexander, Tanvir Bush, Ross Cogan, Joanne Connolly,
Emma Donoghue, Theodore Gayer-Anderson, Peter George,
Gareth Lawless, Eileen McAuley, Nick Midgley, Brian Mitchell,
Imogen Murphy, Toby Radford, Sarah Sarkhel, Gregory Sly,
James Williams.